# JACK PARLETT

## Same Blue, Different You

BROKEN SLEEP BOOKS

Published 2020,
Broken Sleep Books:
Cornwall / Wales

brokensleepbooks.com

Paperback Edition

Lay out your unrest.

Publisher/Editor: Aaron Kent

Typeset in UK by Aaron Kent

Broken Sleep Books is committed to
a sustainable future for our planet,
and therefore uses print on
demand publication.

aaron@brokensleepbooks.com

ISBN: 978-1-913642-02-0

# Contents

*Our bodies are young and blue*
 - Lorde

*Candidly. The past, the sensations of the past. Now!*

 - Frank O'Hara

# Same Blue, Different You

Jack Parlett

# First Name

Orion dithers less, ossified in
Lust and shy, your own app for
Ardour scripted quietly in tongue
On a he's face – you – caught in
Lieu of moonlight, looking blue
Under oath but vivid still under
Water, where names tell of boys
Anciently, and you never told me.

## Lather Near

*Stranger* don't be
vexing order
in the hardened syntax
of missing
    *tu me manques*
while miles numerous
gloat
*like the deserts miss*
      *the rain*
& the question makes
oceanic
as the period stops
        there,
disciples clasping
at night-time ships,
the old hat rules
for forgetting when
*it feels like*
*a mighty*
*long time*
to be living without
succour under shower
heads, fixtures of past
tomorrows sought
      *a l'avenir*
in passing;

the same blue
a different you

and with this our hero
leaps forward
to the street,
an *essai*,

    *shoe-bop shoe-bop.*

# *Trade*

'Make me believe in you' – a lavender
throated plaint takes lodge in the cheek
of the jocund punter, sweet for all that's
capaciously to come (on my face) not
failing to plug the Technicolor residue
of august simplicity. I am mother of this
house, preparing clock-faces for close-ups,
arranging crystals of the heart's salt to cure
your queer return. I sip from the ode
of the ritually dejected, impure glamour
of the cruising fairies. Rouged and quartered
you follow me to an empty dive sick
with play, where the twinks are departed
and the jockstraps cannot hold, where
we cannot know the otters from the bears.
However slick your handshake, bodies
are not your empire.

## Playlist

Near your hotel room cries learnt the buildings
when freely we wandered a temporary city in wait
for the end, to wave off the cab, misled by ballads

in Grand Central subway, tears and Frank Ocean in ear
behind suns, and one (only one) lady noted with tissues.
I always depended on the blindness of strangers,

and back home in our station chance conjures you brief
and the dust barely settles before pleasantries
you're gone again, and this is what songs are for.

## Gaylord

*for Andrea Leadsom*

Baked beans
school meals
hot dog days
playing ball
& hearing
isn't he a nice
boy, puffed up
and quiet
sensitive even
friends with girls
a 'bookish' type
seen singing
Will Young
by the goalposts
piquing suspicions
among straight
talking mums.
"One day this kid"
camp before his time
will process this hurt
in some queer poetry
workshop. Smiling
will go home to kiss
his boyfriend
in unknown places;
limp-wristed
and ham-fisted
will laugh away
your scorn
through pink
and zealous tears,
bowing in thanks
for the other voices
to which he was
exposed

## Sufficiently Charged

My serenity is no longer alarming:
just light and wired and lacking red
so I chase velvet and blonde
and hunger but find only the cut
in the trinity, the fatty joints
of the search while we pause
in moods before glassy shutters.
What does disappointment
do? It sprouts not blooms and has
its thorns and takes as given
the freshness of enough, re-matching
chore to charm to make a remedy
of the over-indexed, to soothe like the lure
of the plant-based and the sting
of its abandonment, so open-faced
and bookish I go on to go off, fall in
and out of rising to quirks in the rind,
I want to live in credit, the apex
of impossible behaviour, but tardiness
comes in stretches and drains the cline,
flexing dulls loose and honeyed
and at last the pocket buzzes in early
hours with a message: the triple threat.

## Today Years Old

I, encrypted crystal of late,
keep watch as the calendar
sweats in pluralistic orange,
minoring in boiler-house
or post-office blues. The sun
outside is vintage, is dusty, is
definitely not ours. Stay calm
by the green canal window,
they tell us, and give those clothes
a wash. You cannot iron desire,
but the pearl will open anyway,
lodged beneath the bucket hat
of a man you used to know. Feel
the space, how the move from lead
to ink is no substitute for a cool
haircut, holding a smoke or pint
to boot. I shape-shift in cliché,
stay late to linger long, and cut
my teeth on bigger words, the lazy
heritage of our discount days.

## *Volta*

An easy letter or unsimple melody
chained to epics of problematic splendour,
the chequered auspice of remarks
you called cute and I, old-fashioned,
unknowing schedules broke and hard
to keep when claiming rebellion at the drop
of a nib, spent by post-tense stops
and the gay pains of irresponsible being.

I'm newly opened to finding solace west
combing stumbles in the arc of bent
togetherness, our mess, how luggage orients
us otherwise, recovering comforts of the amateur.
Express routes vex the promise, and dead ringers
phone, my voice arching to keep us here, so lone.

# Three Aubades Against Straight Time

### i

To be embodied by anyone, just
anyone, is an unrequited pleasure.
The matte of their chest hair flowers
to welcome other mornings, the light
of prosthetic futures we will spend
in solitude, thinking of how terribly
prone we are to not saying goodbye.

### ii

Just how will the river imagine us?
There can be no embrace without it.
Tidal ages sit in the blink of an eye
and the bite of a nail, while we remain
in the hold of completion: grunting,
screaming, never leaving, suspended
by the heat we were forged from.

### iii

Are you for earth? It's this way please,
straight down the line. The voice crowns
and swells, its sound is filled like a tooth
with metal to usher the dawn of an oral
culture. Standing up, the hard lip seeds
and suddenly we could be anywhere, in
love or latrine, wherever space happens.

## Domestic

What's the weather like in LA? I think of you scrolling
in successive Ubers, dappled by arrogant sun or stopping
for donuts, round joke of a square meal: you, sleeping
and working and pulling from stores across the sprawl,
the mall, and other clichés I can confect to bring us
closer – what time is it there? Drunk, messy-haired,
the hours before your flight from Mean Time, me time,
assemblage of cards and cables forgotten but not lost
as I ride a car, hungover princess of the city's south-east,
from Greenwich, home of you and sometimes me and all
time, where it's Sunday now and I'm walking past
the new IKEA site, the smell of fresh wood and near
completion, and think how slowly it has taken shape,
so big and blue, and so have we – your keys in my pocket.

## O's Jacket
*after Frank O'Hara*

black
puffer, yours, echo
of poofter and other
vintage slurs but you
keen to keep me safe
lend your warm fit
the holding pattern
of workdays to rub
out memory of street
bottles thrown, ensuing
silence with collateral
bonds, when this season
'batty-boy' is the new
'faggot' again, but I
style it, assuming you
and walk daily with it
around my shoulders
no other purpose but
for now

## Jersey Lily

This room is ours now, off-white
set to beach the mess of first tries
in minutes, old starts fit to plural
wardrobes folded purplish. Local
sky lacks seasoning but sings jurassic
desire, domestic visions in open air
for talk of taint and spice. We hide
in more's alcove for sanguine orange
and the tune of darker birds, hoping
for swatches ashed to coast coital
luxe beneath fresh sheets. We feel
in hotel robes the weight of colour,
where I love you means minerally:
clear and suite-like and bottled
at the source, still dreaming.

# *Bankable*

They who broker
their chances
on the gold lay
of hopeful designs
will tend to lose
their hair sooner,
their morals quicker
and, waiting in the sand
of a smiling cashmere
bay, will deliver in spite
their own versions
of the actual.

# Fairy

Cherry pop
washing down

inaugural tastes
of other boys.

A spritz of violet
blonde, to imagine

fairer shapes alone
at dressing tables.

These I wear as retro
wishes, synthetic

vengeance for a sissy
childhood

– a click!

and 'such control of form!'
said Celine Dion to the candy floss
in ersatz revolution, but where
are the field notes for this gum
fantasy? the instructions for how
to be other?

Take a lambda rag
and soak it
in the essence of a rose
gelatinised by rage

then stay to watch
the waxen miracle

an old you in sequins

a dancing martyr
shedding pigment
on the party line.

# Novi

We make our own language to fill
the air of an upstairs terrace, queer
art (after Halberstam) of shouting
or shimmying across benches
to terrify punters and upstarts
alike. It's the music of giving no
fucks and making friends along
the way: Marcus, master of Jinzu,
and Floyd, consummate Daddy
of the races, not forgetting Emma
of the pneumatic chest (happy fortieth
darling) and the rogue hangers-on
who elicit sudden sick. 'No hats
indoors' and 'are you going *home*?'
and 'three Elvis Dogs please', 'how
do you turn the heaters on?' If those
walls could talk they'd shout open
secrets about the radical praxis
of Tuesday nights and the grand
opening of Elio's Tex Mex
on mornings after. Serenaded
by Robyn or Lorde or Charli
we tear around to add glitter
to the glum and gaily know
that things will be the same
tomorrow.

# *A Flare*


is peachy Armie Hammer dancing to The Psychedelic Furs in short
shorts or Adèle Exarchopolous dancing to Lykke Li and Annette Bening
singing to Joni Mitchell or Julianne Moore dancing and singing to
Etta James and it's Chipper Corey dancing and syncing to
Patti's LaBelle's 'Somewhere Over the Rainbow' in a Harlem ball-room
it's Judy Garland and her lineage, it's life as a cabaret and it's sitting alone
in your room watching Cate Blanchett watch Rooney Mara sipping
a martini and it's friends and comrades marching in Paris in 1991
and Mya Taylor marching down Santa Monica Boulevard in 2015
it's not just high Camp or down-low-masc it's being taught to swim by
Mahershala Ali and it's a cigarette shared through a prison glory-hole
it's the way Jason smokes to Shirley Clarke's camera in furs and smiles
it's Tilda Swinton in everything and it's Derek Jarman's everything
it's being busy thinking 'bout boys and beautiful movements queer
cinematic sexiness because what else is flamboyance but the flame
that lights a screen or steals a heart, projections you hold a torch for
because with them you feel found and less alone and in 'times of great
crisis', a great poet of crises once said, 'we must all decide again and again

whom we love', and what else is fandom but deciding who loves us back across
the barrier, as when a train departs like the end of *Weekend* and we wait
for another star, one we haven't met yet, knowing we'll be the better for it –
it's that after years of watching we never call off the search.

## Millennium Edition

Wooden floors gather dust – are you bored
yet? Bedding down you acknowledge the state
of your condition, affording tickets but not
the ride home, cherry on top of epochal
lessons sought greenly in residence. We all
take the sign of how to advance; foreground
al fresco in the rush for empty tables. Souls
sit at the bottom of a sour – pop – and power
to the dreamers chasing regret in equinotical
doses, frostier than thou atop charm's summit.
I, for one, welcome the task of such shallow
waters. But that's me, an intellectual, greasy
haired in finery, a phoned-in friend, ready
and waiting for the bridge to open.

## Pair Shaped

Honey dropped mild hurts – a mood – the grinning
saliva of gods who un-birth stars at a song's remove.

I like my emotions farm to table and my metaphors
like my men, ethical but messy, and above all available.

Charred, active and seeking healing, in jest you chase
freedom to the tryst, the lonely fuck that baked the salt in.

I see myself in unkind squares, new ratios, bland escapes
from poorer traits and the wish to be fat with assurance.

Heeding the lesson of want, you act sweeter in the face
of mistrust, craft melancholia, see the marbling mid-rift.

It's the sole condition, seeking affections on the nose
to tail, squashing bigger pictures with their unkempt plots.

To this we both are sentenced, the unsavoury collective
shrug, calling time on the instant we are best before.

# My Hands on Your Body

*after David Wojnarowicz*

How to distract the body from its work
and yours, from silent needs laying still
and nude, hard-as-nails made manifest
in blush. Our little past: I'd trim pieces off you
forgive. Today the lid of your lotion jar
cracked clean and glassy at the temple
of self-improvement, a clink in the communal
showers, no joining fee, gift of life in a golden
shopping complex, pressed to join the ranks
of the visible and feel the cut of silver, crimson
wetness expressed by tissue. It will glisten, like us,
with traces of the rawest instinct, the lights
of broken indicators. They flicker to the tune,
unknown by metronome, of one corporeal song.

## *Showroom*

If you need reminding of how to remember
then catch me concave or convex in sepia
tones. Learn to watch yourself with candour
in the glass of a kiln, lit only by the blush
of a forgotten moon; the stuff of the past
composed in the style of a different tongue.
Listen carefully for the abject spark, a stray
cough crackling amid the sullen order of lunar
shelves. It's the lesson of habitation: to hear
the lumpen silence of familiar *milieus*, shuffling
about in the breathed-on foreground of domestic
mockery. At least you'll be schooled in proper
shapes; will know what it is to hold, or was.

# *Ensemble, Ensemble*

Ask a poem of its trade and it replies
'imperatives', telling you to 'just do it!'
To stare that second longer, to catch the later train
or list your first kisses – we all have more than one
of those. You can pad along fine without field notes,
but the twilights will surely be different, more certain,
fewer flowers. You know already that attention is precious,
but don't we need an extra shove to see the beauty
of handsome boys who kiss their grandmothers
goodbye; of the changes wrought by a year upon
your own terrain; to see sentiments lacking style,
gossamer falling saccharine. Cold sweat runs slowly
and instructions will not save us, nor menthols
from the ban, though they too mix death with aroma.
We know only this: that Happy Hour is unassailable,
that curiosity in another is not *for another hour, but this
hour. Not for another place, but this place.* So tell me
the secrets of your glassiness and the hairiness within you,
as though it made a difference.

## Campe-Toi

See that boy and his hyacinth rigour, dancing
at the edges of the acceptable under belvedere
rain. Beneath the hot lights he does not sing
to appease this scene; those who do not hear
a voice, twinkling, simply sit. Bohemia claps
and gammon stomachs turn when knowing
that the garlands are his, as he moving maps
the world so other to pints of milk, owing
nothing but choreography. He changes foot
to redistribute the weight of alone unlearning
how we told him to be, the new art of the put
down, to make the clandestine public, yearning
in character with an icy smile. Is he foolish or
brave? The word you've looked your life for.

## Any Other Name

Now being here it's modern love
Or else, after a grey sleep a plow
Raised is a plow shared, where I'll
Mild try to forget you on Meeker
And shelter in excess lip wishing
Night to come at the intersection.

Meat products on Moffat and comfort on
Ice, eau de bodega, sullen bush & lit wick so
Kindly he hosts for rolling deep by the L
Entraining to be held while the party begins.

'Move on already' means chasing
Indented kisses without knowing,
Change for a tip to keep it going
Heat and quiet will lead you there
After more tokes for a touch you
Expect from a face on the block,
Let's dance, in A's un-filtered air.

Green and under a wing for leather
Red lights and dirt of a cruel scene to
Exhale in being watched, the naked
Gaiety stiffed with him as my guide.

Excavating hopes of what will come to
Be archives you out, old replies danced
Interior reeling for feeling fragile for the
Tea he is spilling without a thought for the
Intimacies he sub-lets from you in time.

# *Notes*

The epigraphs are taken from Lorde's song 'Hard Feelings' (*Melodrama*, 2017) and Frank O'Hara's long poem 'Second Avenue' (1953).

The poems 'First Name' and 'Any Other Name' are both acrostics.

'Lather Near' interpolates lyrics from the songs 'Missing' by Everything But the Girl (*Amplified Heart*, 1994) and 'Hello Stranger' by Barbara Lewis (*Hello Stranger*, 1963).

'A Flare' describes moments from the following films: *Call Me By Your Name* (dir. Luca Guadagnino, 2017), *Blue is the Warmest Colour* (dir. Abdellatif Kechiche, 2013), *The Kids Are All Right* (dir. Lisa Cholodenko, 2010), *A Single Man* (dir. Tom Ford, 2009), *Paris Is Burning* (dir. Jennie Livingston, 1990), *Cabaret* (dir. Bob Fosse, 1972), *120 BPM* (dir. Robin Campillo, 2017), *Tangerine* (dir. Sean Baker, 2015), *Moonlight* (dir. Barry Jenkins, 2016), *Portrait of Jason* (dir. Shirley Clarke, 1967) and *Weekend* (dir. Andrew Haigh, 2011).

The phrase "princess of the city's south-east" in the poem 'Domestic' is inspired by a similar title given to me by my dear friend Charlotte Barrington on the morning in question.

# Acknowledgments

My thanks to the editors of the magazines where some of these poems have previously appeared:

*BFI Flare LGBTQ+ Festival Zine* ('A Flare')
*Hotel* ('Trade', 'My Hands on Your Body', 'Volta', 'Sufficiently Charged')
*Visual Verse* ('Showroom')

'Gaylord' was awarded Second Prize in the Verve Poetry Festival Competition 2020 and was published in the accompanying anthology, *We've Done Nothing Wrong. We've Nothing to Hide* (Verve Poetry Press, 2020)

*LAY OUT YOUR UNREST*

Lightning Source UK Ltd.
Milton Keynes UK
UKHW021836040920
369356UK00005B/359